Meet Me at the FAIR

Meet Me at the FAIR

County, State, and World's Fairs & Expositions

By Judy Alter

A FIRST BOOK

Franklin Watts

A Division of Grolier Publishing

New York • London • Hong Kong • Sydney
Danbury, Connecticut

Photo credits ©: Archive Photos: 12, 28, 42, 51; Buffalo Bill Historical Center, Cody, WY: 48; Chicago Historical Society: 46, 49; Corbis-Bettmann: 11, 13, 14, 15, 17, 32, 33, 34, 35, 37, 40, 43, 44 top, 50; Culver Pictures: 10, 22, 44 inset; The Image Works: 29 (Carini), 8, 9 (Daemmrich), 57 top (Dratch), 25 top (Granitsas), cover top left (Larry Kolvoord), cover bottom right, 2 (McLaughlin), 56 bottom right (Okoniewski), 31 (Lee Snider); Iowa State Fair: 25 bottom, 26, 57 inset; J.W. Westerfield: 30, 56 top; Minnesota Historical Society: 19, 20, 21; North Wind Picture Archives: 36, 38; Superstock, Inc: 54; U.T. Institute of Texan Cultures: 16.

Library of Congress Cataloging-in-Publication Data
Alter, Judy.
    Meet me at the fair! : county, state, and world's fairs and expositions /by Judy Alter
       p.   cm – (A first book)
    Includes bibliographical references and index.
    Summary: Presents a history of fairs, from early livestock shows to county and state fairs and international expositions and world's fairs.
    ISBN 0-531-20307-7
    1. Fairs–History–Juvenile literature. 2. Exhibitions–History–Juvenile literature. [1. Fairs–History. 2. Exhibitions–History.] I. Title. II. Series.
HF5471.A55 1997
394'.6–dc21   97-5700
                                                           CIP
                                                           AC

1 2 3 4 5 6 7 8 9 10 R 06 05 04 03 02 01 00 99 98 97

Contents

5

ONE

History of the Fair

In October 1996, nearly three and a half million people visited the State Fair of Texas in Dallas–that's more than 150,000 people each day during the fair's three-week run. They ate **corn dogs** and rode the Ferris wheel and roller coasters, watched 4-H youngsters show prize cattle with pride and then turn teary-eyed when a steer was sold for slaughter, gazed at rows of homemade pies, cakes, and relishes in the women's hall, marveled at huge and expensive machinery in the agricultural hall, listened to music from rock groups and high school marching bands,

and from soloists and groups presenting the music of every nationality. Exhausted, they ended a long day by watching spectacular fireworks displays. Not one of these weary fairgoers probably ever heard of Elkanah Watson.

In 1807, New York businessman, banker, and gentleman farmer Elkanah Watson wanted a good wool supply for his New England woolen mills. He decided the way to interest other farmers in raising fine sheep might be to exhibit his own two merino sheep—a Spanish breed known for producing a wool of high quality. So in the town of Pittsfield, in the Berkshire area of Massachusetts, Watson paraded his sheep around the town square. Surprised and greatly pleased by the

8

"Big Tex," the symbol of
the Texas State Fair

attention paid to the two sheep, Watson began to wonder if more animals would attract even more attention. He talked with some of the farmers who had gathered around his sheep, and they agreed to show their animals.

Watson spent the next three years promoting the raising of livestock. By 1810 he had interested twenty-six of his neighbors in an event he called the Berkshire Cattle Show. Some of the farmers were afraid they would be laughed at as they paraded their cattle. Watson stepped forward to lead the way, and the other farmers followed to parade their livestock around the town square. At the end of the parade, Watson recalled, he gave "three cheers, in which they all united" and then they parted, "well pleased with the day, and with each other."

The next year, 1811, the newly incorporated Berkshire Agricultural Society sponsored the livestock show. This time, the gathering had some new features. A prize of $70 was offered for the best animals, turning the event into a competition rather than just an exhibition. A

Livestock exhibits have been a central feature of the county fair from the first fairs to the present.

County fair competitions: Which is the strongest team of working oxen?

speech was introduced, and Watson himself spoke, emphasizing patriotism, describing "this good land," and stressing the need for all to work together.

For this 1811 parade, each marcher wore a hat decorated with a cockade—two small heads of wheat tied with thread. The officers of the agricultural society wore cockades made of three heads of wheat tied with green ribbon. Oxen pulled a plow, and two stagecoaches were added to the parade, one carrying a loom and a spinning jenny (an advanced spinning wheel or early spinning machine that had more than one spindle, thus allowing a person to spin more than one thread at a time). The show had moved beyond a simple livestock exhibition.

Each year, the fair grew. In 1812, prizes for "women's domestic manufacture" were added, but local women were reluctant to attend to receive their prizes. Watson had to get his own wife to come first and then sent a messenger to tell the others that Mrs. Watson was in attendance. By 1813 seventeen prizes were awarded to agriculture, twenty to livestock, fifteen to women's domestic manufacture—fabric, clothing, and perhaps

Who can guess the weight of a champion pig?

A county fair in the 1870s, with a horse auction and a balloon ascension

food—and eleven to men's domestic manufacture—no doubt such things as furniture and tools. A grand agricultural ball closed the exhibition. Watson remembered that "many farmers' daughters graced the [dance] floor," to music supplied by local fiddlers.

The idea of gathering together to show off livestock was not original. Fairs of this sort had been common in Europe for centuries, having begun often as religious festivals. But in the United States, Watson is generally considered the father of agricultural fairs because he took the idea far beyond the display of cattle. Agricul-

14

tural societies in neighboring counties soon followed what became known as the Berkshire plan—farmers would pay small dues to the society and receive a certificate of membership. The fees helped to produce the annual agricultural fair which, through the interest it awakened and the prizes it awarded, encouraged farmers to try to produce bigger, better crops. Livestock and agricultural shows spread throughout New England, New York, and parts of the South and the Midwest.

In this country today only a relatively small number of people earn their living by farming. But in the 1850s— the years just before the Civil War—farming was America's most important occupation. The farmers needed to know how to raise better cattle, grow more crops, and use the latest machinery, and looked for advice on other agricultural matters. Agricultural associations served as schoolrooms for them, where they could learn new techniques and share information. By the late 1850s there were agri-

"Going to the Fair," an 1876 engraving

A meeting of the local agricultural society in Cat Spring, Texas, 1884

cultural societies or boards in twenty-five states. Most held annual fairs.

Education and improvement in farming techniques may have been the main goal, but most fair promoters and producers knew that these events also offered family recreation. For many farm families, the fair was the only chance in the year that they had to get off the farm and have some fun. Fair managements hired amusement acts, and the tradition of the **midway** began, with food and trinkets for sale, **sideshows**, a merry-go-round or carousel, wild animal shows, freak shows, magicians, and fortune tellers. In the late 1800s, horse racing was often added to the entertainments available at a fair. Perhaps because of the horse races—and the betting that sometimes accompanied them—rumors and wild gossip often flew through the towns where fairs were held. They hinted at shady activities or, at the very least, dealings not according to the standards of proper people—but still the fairs drew big crowds.

An 1888 county fair poster

TWO

The Palaces

In the 1880s, some fair managements built elaborate palaces, designed after medieval castles, to attract crowds. These palaces were constructed from whatever material was special in the local area. In Minnesota, it was an ice palace; in Iowa, a corn palace; in Texas, a building made of native grasses and plants.

The city of Saint Paul, Minnesota, had enjoyed several years of growth and progress by 1886. To celebrate, city leaders formed the Saint Paul Winter **Carnival** Association and chose a site on which to erect an ice palace

A "Blanket Toss" game in front of The Ice Palace at the Saint Paul Winter Carnival, 1887

The Ice Palace
at night

such as one built in the eighteenth century for the empress of Russia and another built more recently in Montreal, Canada. The palace was planned for the center of the Crystal Carnival, which would also feature a display of seventy-five Sioux Indians, an exhibition hall, a baseball diamond, toboggan rides, and rinks for skating, polo, lacrosse and curling (a nineteenth-century version of hockey).

The palace, built of square blocks of ice cemented together with water, featured a massive square tower, smaller round towers at each corner, with battlements or raised walls capping all the towers, and four grand, arched entrances. It was a full-scale palace, not a playhouse. One observer described it as a "magnificent pile of glittering ice, when seen beneath the bright rays of the winter sun, or at night when illuminated by white electric lights and fires of varied hues."

In the following years, the Crystal Carnival grew larger, and the ice palaces grander, with turrets or small towers, large, external supports called buttresses, and huge sculptures. In 1887, there were two rival castles.

The Corn Palace at the Iowa State Fair in Sioux City

The larger boasted a ladies' retiring room, a hot lunch room, a warming room with a fireplace (one wonders that it didn't melt the ice!), an oyster room, a gentlemen's coat room, a gallery, and a bandstand. In 1888 the castle was the scene of a wedding with 6,000 guests.

In the first two years, the festival featured "stormings," or attacks on the castle, complete with fireworks. But in 1888 the temperature rose into the forties; the palace began to melt, and the fireworks were too soggy to ignite. For the next two years, also, the weather was too warm during December and January to build an ice palace. After that the city lost enthusiasm for the project. In the end, the ice palaces were defeated by the temperature.

In Sioux City, Iowa, a corn palace was built to celebrate the growth of the city—and an especially good corn crop. When the palace opened in October 1887, the entire city was decorated with corn.

Fair organizers in Fort Worth, Texas, designed the Spring Palace, a huge fairy-castle-like building with many turrets and towers. Inside and out, the castle was decorated with the products of Texas—wheat, corn stalks, cactus, moss, rye, Johnson grass, cotton, dried straw, even popcorn and peas. One evening in its second season, the building, with about 7,000 people inside, was suddenly swept by fire. No one knows the origin of the fire, although some say a young boy, happily dancing, stepped on a match and set off a spark. Because of all the dried grasses, the Spring Palace quickly filled with flames. Within eleven minutes it burned to the ground. Miraculously, only one life was lost: Al Hayne, a civil engineer who made many trips into the burning building to rescue others. Today a monument to Hayne stands near the site of the Spring Palace in downtown Fort Worth.

THREE

The Fair Today

Although they began as agricultural shows, state and regional fairs are flourishing in today's urban society, providing both agricultural education for city dwellers and entertainment for families. Attendance at most fairs increases each year, in spite of fears that gambling **casinos** will take people elsewhere for their entertainment. Fairs are such a big business today—providing educational displays and entertainment to millions—that they have their own trade association, the

The small animal barn at a county fair in upstate New York

The lion tamer show, Iowa State Fair

A rock concert
at a state fair

International Association of Fairs and Expositions, with headquarters in Springfield, Missouri. The IAFE provides seminars, management courses, surveys, publications, and an annual trade show. The association also monitors bills, regulations, and mandates pertaining to fairs, in Washington, D.C.

In addition to the IAFE, there are smaller associations in more than forty states. The New York Association of Agricultural Fairs drew 1,200 participants to its 105th annual convention in the early 1990s. Fairgoers who simply go to fairs to tour the exhibits, listen to the music, and eat the food, often are unaware that in just one state, 1,200 people may be involved in producing agricultural fairs—not one fair but many—and that this has been going on for over a hundred years.

Fair managers hope for large attendance figures and they know that two things affect the size of the crowds: weather, which is beyond their control, and entertainment, which they can control to the extent their budgets permit. When the weather is sunny, crowds are big; when it rains, attendance is down. Show managers simply cross their fingers and hope. But the better the entertainment, the bigger the names, the larger the crowd. Lucky is the fair that can advertise Willie Nelson and Family as featured entertainers, or Clint Black, Wynonna Judd, Bob Dylan, or Barry Manilow. The range of entertainment offered at shows is almost unbelievable. A troupe of thirteen performing dogs, known as the Mess of Mutts, performs at as many as twenty events a year. Other fairs feature stock car races, performing pigs, bicycle and in-line skating stunt shows, reptile exhibits, and strolling entertainers. If it will attract a crowd, you can almost bet it's been tried as entertainment at some fair, somewhere.

The midway, past...

No show or fair is complete without the carnival or midway, with its rides, booths, sideshows, and corn dogs. Operators of these colorful carnivals—often called by the uncomplimentary name of "carny people"—travel from fair to fair; the fees they pay to the fair management make up one of the principal sources of income for many fairs. And they can be the most expensive part of the fair for many visitors. The midway seems especially exciting to some visitors, with its freewheeling atmosphere.

...and present.

Some agricultural and livestock groups sponsor national or regional shows that are primarily devoted to their product, rather than covering the whole range of rural productions, as seen at state fairs. The most common are livestock shows. The Southwestern **Exposition** and Livestock Show of Fort Worth, Texas, which celebrated its centennial in 1996, is typical. Once called the Fat Stock Show, it began in 1886, when a few local ranchers tied their prize cattle to some trees near a local

A horse parade at the Southwestern Exposition and Livestock Show

Clowns and rodeo events at the Southwestern Exposition

river to exhibit them. Today the three-week event attracts 800,000 people, features one of the most important **rodeos** in the country, and draws exhibitors from all over the country. Cattle are still king at the exposition, but horses are also shown, along with rabbits, pigeons, swine, sheep, mules, and such **exotics** as emus and ostriches. Tradespeople exhibit everything from livestock fencing and recreational vehicles, to turquoise jewelry and machines that chop vegetables. The midway roars with life far into the night, and vendors offer corn dogs, **cotton candy**, and **funnel cakes**. For many Texans in small towns, the livestock show is the event of the year.

At various times, this country has seen and still sees shows devoted to dairy animals, swine, poultry, exotic animals, cotton, corn, and so on. County fairs are less important now than when more people depended on farming for their living. But many counties still hold fall fairs, often in small but permanent fairgrounds, and give prizes for agricultural products. These fairs are important because they give youngsters more chances to compete than do the larger fairs.

Competing for livestock honors at a county fair

FOUR

World's Fairs and Expositions

*C*ounty and regional fairs led to world's fairs and expositions, which are really just bigger and better fairs—but with different subject matter.

Although large displays and spectacles call themselves world's fairs today, the true world's fair, which demonstrates the way of life of the period which produces it, is a thing of the past. Between 1850 and 1925, there was at least one major inter-

A house-furnishings exhibit in the great exhibition hall at the 1851 London fair

national exhibition held somewhere in the world each year, and in several years, there was more than one fair. The formula for these fairs was simple: instead of showing advances in farming methods and the raising of animals, they were showcases for industrial displays, new inventions, the discoveries of science and technology that were rapidly changing daily life. A world's fair offered the host city a chance to look at itself and what was happening to it as technology advanced.

The first true world's fair was held in Hyde Park,

London, England, in 1851. Queen Victoria opened the fair, which celebrated the changes brought about by industry and business. Other fairs followed in Paris, France; Vienna, Austria; Brussels, Belgium; Antwerp and Amsterdam, Holland; Sidney and Melbourne, Australia. These were city fairs, unlike the county fairs which celebrated farming achievements, and they promoted national rivalry. A country sponsored a fair to show off its advancements and its ambition.

If it did not produce the first world's fair, the United States did produce the greatest number of these exhi-

The Crystal Palace at the 1853 fair in New York City

Erecting the great Corliss engine in Machinery Hall at the 1876 Centennial Exhibition in Philadelphia

bitions between 1850 and 1925. The first United States Fair was held in New York City in 1853 and was a clear imitation of the British fair. Even though the fair was produced by P. T. Barnum of Barnum & Bailey Circus fame, it was a flop. There were only a few foreign exhibitors, and attendance was low at this "Exhibition of the Industry of All Nations."

In 1876 Philadelphia produced a **centennial** celebration—one-hundred years after the Declaration of Independence. This was a fair on a grand scale. President

Ulysses S. Grant opened the event. There were 150 buildings, with exhibitors from the various states and territories (Arizona was not yet a state) and from foreign countries. Eight million visitors toured 30,000 exhibits from 32 countries. The focus was on machines: Alexander Graham Bell's new telephone (there were only 3,000 in the world), the Westinghouse air brake, Edison's telegraph, the typewriter, the refrigerated railroad car, the sewing machine, and—the center of attention—the gigantic steam-powered Corliss engine. Weighing 800 tons, it sent power to 8,000 different machines in the building.

In June 1876, bands of Sioux and Cheyenne warriors

The Art Gallery of the U.S. Centennial Exhibition

An 1895 drawing entitled: "President Grover Cleveland visiting the Negro Building at the Cotton States and International Exposition," Atlanta, Georgia

met U.S. army forces led by George Armstrong Custer at the Little Big Horn River in Montana. Custer's entire force was killed in this last victory of the Plains Indians. The battle of Little Big Horn and the deaths of Custer and his troops were still fresh in the public memory. That sad episode dimmed people's enjoyment of the fair and also colored the exhibit dealing with American Indian. They were shown as small, cruel, and bloodthirsty. The exhibition was narrow in other ways, too: only two black artists were represented, and there was no exhibit showing the contribution of black people to the nation's hundred-year history.

Women were included in the planning of the exposition only as an afterthought, and many saw the Women's Pavilion as insulting because it was small and failed to deal with the most important problem of women at that time: the struggle for equal rights under the law.

Running from May until November, the Philadelphia exposition drew the largest attendance of any fair held in the United States to that time. Other fairs followed, some small, some major. The Pan American Exposition in Buffalo, New York, in 1901 was marked by the fact that President William McKinley was assassinated there.

Most major fairs, like the Philadelphia celebration, marked some historic event or geographic region: The

The Louisiana Purchase Exposition of 1904 included a futuristic view of exploration under and over the sea and demonstrations of traditional Native American crafts.

New Orleans World's Industrial and Cotton Exposition and the Atlanta Cotton States and International Exposition (1895); the Tennessee Centennial Exposition (Nashville, 1897); the Trans Mississippi and International Exposition in Omaha, Nebraska (1898); the South Carolina Interstate and West Indian Exposition (1901-2); the Louisiana Purchase Exposition in Saint Louis, Missouri (1904); the Lewis and Clark Centennial and Asian Pacific Exposition and Oriental Fair in Portland, Oregon (1905); the Jamestown (Virginia) Tercentenary Exposition (1907); the Alaska-Yukon-Pacific Exposition in Seattle, Washington (1909); the Panama/Pacific International Exposition in San Francisco (1915), celebrating the opening of the Panama Canal; and the Panama/California Exposition in San Diego in 1915-1916. But the most important was the World's Columbian Exposition in Chicago in 1893.

An exposition to celebrate the four hundredth anniversary of Columbus's arrival in the Western Hemisphere was mentioned as early as the mid-1880s, and several cities–Saint Louis, New York, Washington, D.C., and others–made serious application to host the event. In April 1890, President William Henry Harrison signed laws providing for an "International Exhibition of Arts, Industries, Manufactures, and the Products of the Soil, Mine and Sea, in the City of Chicago." Planning began immediately.

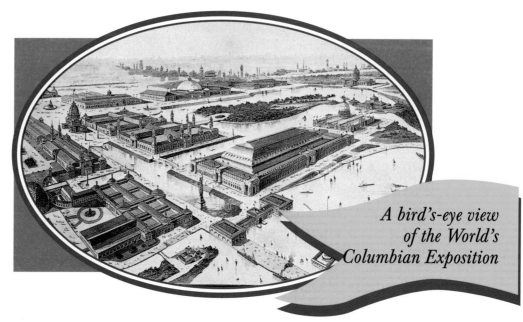

A bird's-eye view of the World's Columbian Exposition

The exposition buildings were erected on land mostly in the city's public park system—Washington and Jackson parks on the south side, connected by the Midway Plaisance, a narrow mile-long strip of open land that ran just to the south of the University of Chicago. Much of the land was swampy and undeveloped, requiring land fill and landscaping; but when the organizers were finished, exposition buildings stood in the middle of a series of lagoons, basins, and ponds. The Court of Honor, often called the "White City," was a group of white buildings designed in classical style—large, even monumental buildings of balanced design, resembling the temples of ancient Greece and Rome. The buildings were highly decorated and ornamented with columns and pillars, stone carvings, various stone finishes, curving arches, domed roofs, and freestanding statues. Included in the White City were the Administration Building, Machinery Hall, the Agricultural Building, the **Manufactures** and Liberal Arts buildings, the Mines and Mining Building, and Electricity Hall. These buildings were designed by the most famous architects of the day, including Louis Sullivan and August St. Gaudens. They circled the Grand Basin, a long lagoon or shallow pond, containing oversize pieces of sculpture–plunging horses, dolphins, eagles, and fountains. The Court of Honor, wired for electrical display, was connected to other sections of the exposition by terraces,

The White City

At the Midway Plaisance: A parade of "Wild West Indians," and a Bedouin dance performance

canals, walkways, and bridges. It was a magnificent and awe-inspiring sight.

Most states and many foreign countries—from Lapland to Persia, Ireland to Java—were represented by smaller buildings. The State of Virginia, for instance, erected a copy of President George Washington's home at Mount Vernon. There were also buildings devoted to women, children, photography, horticulture, transportation, the arts, and on down a long list. There were gambling casinos and restaurants, a confectionery, a Japanese tea house, and hundreds of other attractions.

The main purpose of the exposition was to offer a serious display of American achievement. The many exhibits were accompanied by congresses or public meetings that focused on the sciences, arts, religion, education, social sciences–all designed to show off intellectual activity in America. There was a World Peace Congress; congresses on architecture, philosophy, labor, and education; and a Women's Congress. The recognition of women's issues was, in fact, one of the major accomplishments of the Columbian Exposition, and some say it opened the way for the women's movement of the last half of the twentieth century.

As was fitting for its serious purpose, the exposition attracted the great thinkers and celebrated persons of the day–Henry Adams, who would write of the exposition in his important book, *The Education of Henry Adams*; historian Frederick Jackson Turner, whose theories on the frontier were to shape over half a century of American history; Jane Addams, who founded Hull House, a pioneer institution offering social services to the poor and needy; suffragist Elizabeth Cady Stanton;

poet Harriet Monroe; and novelist Hamlin Garland.

At the other end of the scale from these serious and learned congresses was the Midway. Intended for displays from various cultures, it was a hodgepodge of people, all in their native dress, offering such entertainments as donkey and camel rides, a trained animal exhibit, a Bedouin village, a Cairo street bazaar, a balloon ride, and a concert hall for music, juggling, and dancing performances. But the main attraction on the Midway was the Ferris wheel.

This invention of George Washington Gale Ferris

The Ferris wheel at the World's Columbian Exposition

was first introduced at the exposition. Two wheels, 264 feet in diameter, held suspended between them 36 cars, each capable of holding 60 people. Fully loaded, this gigantic wheel could carry over 2,000 people. An engine of 2,000 horsepower turned the wheel in a complete revolution every ten minutes. From the top of the wheel, riders had a full view of the exposition grounds and, beyond, the city of Chicago.

Later, some people said the Midway taught Americans how to be joyfully happy and have a good time. Certainly it gave its name forever to the familiar strips at fairs which today house carnival rides, games of chance, and other amusements.

Outside the gates to the exposition, more entertainment was offered. William F. Cody, better known as Buffalo Bill, was not invited to be a regular participant. But he set up his Wild West–he never used the term "show"– just outside the gates and did a booming business in what Chicago Mayor Carter Harrison declared was a "frontier town." Other entertainments joined Cody on the fringes of respectability. In Philadelphia, seventeen years earlier, fair officials persuaded the city to burn down the freak shows and **honky-tonks** that had sprung up outside the gates because they were thought not proper enough to be in the exposition. But Mayor Harrison knew the value of a good show and encouraged them.

"The Attack on the Stagecoach," and the audience at Buffalo Bill's Wild West

The exposition opened with great ceremony on May 1, 1893, and ran through October 31. When it closed, twenty-one and a half million people had paid admission to enter. Estimates are that between 5 and 10 percent of the American population attended at one time or another.

After the exposition was over, Chicago took its place as a major city in America. Nearly destroyed by the Great Fire of 1871, and often scorned as lacking in natural beauty (on flat plains bordering a flat lake), and boasting too much violence (a saloon on every corner), Chicago was the fourth largest city in the United States at the time. By staging a successful fair and doing so while earning a slight profit, the city had proved what it could do. Never again would it feel inferior to Saint Louis, Washington, D.C., or any of its other rivals. Chicago held another world's fair, the Century of Progress Exposition, in 1933. It, too, earned a small profit and brought

The Avenue of Flags at the 1933 Century of Progress Exposition in Chicago

The Trylon and Perisphere, symbols of the 1939 New York World's Fair

more attention to Chicago, but it never reached the greatness of the Columbian Exposition.

One of the most important international fairs of the twentieth century was the World's Fair of New York in 1939. The timing of this two-year show was important—it fell between the end of the Great Depression and the entrance of the United States into World War II, at a time when Europe was already at war. The fair was held in what was called America's Number One City. New York had the tallest buildings, the most restaurants, the largest theater in the world, the most trade. It had the Empire State Building, Rockefeller Center, the RCA

Building and the Rainbow Room, Radio City Music Hall and the Rockettes, eight major newspapers, and three major-league baseball teams. No city in the country could rival New York.

The fairgrounds were built on a tidal backwater, a mosquito-infested garbage dump three miles long and one mile wide in some places. Today people still remember the 1939 fair for its streamlined modern architecture. It boasted the Trylon, a three-sided, 610-foot-tall tower that was higher than the Washington Monument, and the Perisphere, an eighteen-story-high empty shell

The Futurama exhibit, New York World's Fair

set in a shallow pool. Both were gleaming white, dramatic sights.

The fair showed visitors a world of the future—the world we live in today. Television was new, but RCA predicted a big future for it. Long-distance phone calls were unusual, fluorescent lighting was new, and fax machines were barely hinted at. The General Motors Futurama transported visitors in moving chairs, which gave the illusion of flying, to the world of the 1960s. There they saw a seven-lane highway, fruit trees growing under great glass jars (the hothouse tomatoes of today), glass skyscrapers, atomic energy, air conditioning, enormous amusement parks. When visitors came out of the Futurama, they were given buttons that read "I have seen the future." The future they saw was big and bold and colorful. It predicted that people would move to suburbs and the automobile would take over our world and remake our landscape. Fair visitors loved it.

FIVE

The Decline of Expositions

The day of the grand expositions ended after World War II, in the late 1940s. Today we have expositions and hemisfairs and other attractions, but none are built on as grand a scale as the pre-World War II events.

In recent years, some cities have used a world's fair and exposition to improve their images. In 1964 New York held a second exposition on the site of the 1939 event. San Antonio, Texas, attracted six and a half million people to its 1968 Hemisfair. The event helped San

Today's theme parks such as Disney World, and thrill-filled amusement parks, have their origins in yesterday's county and state fairs, and industrial and world expositions.

Antonio become a major tourist city. By the 1990s the city was attracting over ten million visitors a year to its River Walk, the historic Alamo, and special tourist events. In recent years, fairs have become international. Almost every year there is an exposition somewhere in the world, but these lack the grandeur and majesty of the great expositions of the past–the Columbian, the 1939 in Chicago.

There are several possible reasons why expositions are no longer as great. One is cost: although the two expositions in Chicago and the 1939 event in New York earned small profits, most expositions lost money. The aim never was to earn quick money, but rather to improve business over a long period of time by drawing attention to the city. Still, most cities were unable to fund the initial multimillion dollar cost, let alone absorb a loss. The 1933 Chicago fair, for instance, cost $47 million and earned a profit of only $700,000. Congressional funds supported most expositions, and the Smithsonian Institution was heavily involved in developing programs for early expositions. But in spite of this help, expositions were a drain on the host city.

Expositions were criticized all along as being creations of the Anglo upper middle class, and for either not representing or distorting the historical contributions of women and minorities such as African Americans, Latinos, Native Americans, and Asians. The criticism began when black contributions were barely included in the Centennial Exposition, and it continued at the Columbian Exposition when demonstrations of various cultures–Egyptian dancers (popularly called belly dancers in the United States), for instance–were confined to the Midway rather than given a **pavilion**. The New York exposition was criticized as presenting

a way of life that was far beyond the income of most Americans at the time. Rather than showing American life as it really was, critics said, the expositions showed an upper-middle-class view of how life should be.

Fairs today are an exciting mix of American history, enterprise, and energy.

But World War II may also account for the decline of expositions. It has been said that after that great war Americans never again saw themselves as carefree and happy, never again had unlimited faith in the future. And expositions, after all, were about the wonderful future that lay ahead for all of us. It may be that Americans stopped believing in the dream.

Still others point to the development of such larger-than-life amusement parks as Disney World or Disneyland or Six Flags as a cause for the decline of expositions. The Columbian Exposition has been credited with starting the amusement industry in this country, leading to today's theme parks. The link is certainly clear, if for nothing more than the midway and the Ferris wheel, both characteristics of today's amusement parks. Some people suggest that the great expositions have been replaced by these enormous amusement parks that feature the same major attraction—a contained world offering education and amusement, exactly what the expositions offered.

The great expositions may be a thing of the past, but state and county fairs live on as purely American entertainment. Next time there's one near you, go on out and look at the livestock, eat some popcorn, ride the Ferris wheel, and think about Elkanah Watson and his merino sheep. Only in America!

Special Terms

carnival - a traveling amusement show, with shooting galleries, games of chance, and rides such as the Ferris wheel and the merry-go-round

casino - a building used for meetings; the term usually associated with buildings used for gambling

centennial - celebrating a 100-year anniversary

corn dogs, cotton candy, and funnel cakes - typical carnival or fair food: a corn dog is a hot dog in a cornbread batter, fried and served on a stick; cotton candy is sugar, usually colored pink or some other pastel, spun to the consistency of cotton fiber; funnel cakes are fried cakes made from batter dripped into hot oil through a funnel. It's all gooey, bad for you and delicious!

exotics - something really unusual; in early fairs, an exhibition of exotics was often called a freak show and might include a fat lady, a tattooed man, a midget, a sword swallower. Freak shows are not common today because they focus on physical differences

exposition - an exhibit, often of specific products, such as an automobile exposition, an agricultural exposition, a livestock exposition

honky-tonk - a cheap and noisy nightclub; the term is sometimes associated with music played on a tinny-sounding piano

manufactures - products which are manufactured, usually by machines. An exhibition of manufactures might include clothing, household goods, hardware goods

midway - the place at a fair where you find carnival-like amusements, such as games of chance, the Ferris wheel and other rides, and food

pavilion - an open building used for entertainments and exhibitions

rodeo - a show in which participants compete in events patterned after the everyday work of cowboys— bronc riding, calf roping, steer wrestling

sideshow - a less important show performed at the same time as another, bigger show. For example, a circus may have such sideshows as shooting galleries or magicians

tercentenary - celebrating a 300-year anniversary

For More Information

Badger, Reid. *The Great American Fair: The World's Columbian Exposition & American Culture.* Chicago: Nelson Hall, 1979.

Blay, John S. *After the Civil War.* New York: Bonanza Books, 1960.

Gelernter, David. 1939: *The Lost World of the Fair.* New York: Simon & Schuster, 1995.

International Association for Fairs and Expositions. Videotape.

Muccigrosso, Robert. *Celebrating the New World.* Chicago: I. R. Dee, 1993.

Rydell, Robert W. *All the World's a Fair.* Chicago: The University of Chicago Press, 1984.

Index

About the Author

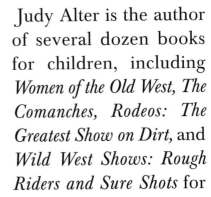

Judy Alter is the author of several dozen books for children, including *Women of the Old West, The Comanches, Rodeos: The Greatest Show on Dirt,* and *Wild West Shows: Rough Riders and Sure Shots* for Franklin Watts. She is the director of Texas Christian University Press, which publishes literature and history of Texas and the American West. Ms. Alter lives in Fort Worth, Texas.